Colors of
Devotion

Colors of Devotion

Carroll Blair

Aveon Publishing Company

ISBN: 978-1-936430-46-8

Library of Congress Control Number
2011902987

Aveon Publishing Co.
P.O. Box 380739
Cambridge, MA 02238-0739 USA

Also by Carroll Blair

Grains of Thought
Facing the Circle
Reel to Real
Shifting Tides
Reaches
Out of Silence
Quarter Notes
By Rays of Light
Into the Inner Life
Gnosis of the Heart
Soul Reflections
Beneath and Beyond the Surface
Of Courage and Commitment
For Today and Tomorrow
In Meditation
Sightings Along the Journey
Through Desert's Fire
Offerings to Pilgrims
Human Natures
(Of Animal and Spiritual)
Atoms from the Suns of Solitude
Voicings
Through the Shadows
As the World Winds Flow

The devotion that will be explored
in the following pages is a devotion
beyond all self-interests, dedicated
to the broadening of spiritual
realization, to living in a manner
that opens the way to the majesty
of higher wisdom and beauty,
working for the removal of barriers
that keep humankind from
inhabiting a greater state of being;
a devotion that takes its faithful
servants as far on the spiritual
path as they are able to go and
of what is gained, to be given in
service for all through ministration
of the life of selfless love.

From the concentrated mind
and consecrated heart comes
the life of devotion.

A rich life is a principled life, not
to be confused with one that spends
lavishly on material luxuries
or flaunts an earthly wealth.

The lives that stand first in the service of humanity are those that lived to serve, not placing themselves first.

Devotion is rooted in love; it
bears its strength through love;
a strength that fosters a will
which sees no sacrifice as too
great to fulfill its mission.

To be constantly serving the world
in a selfless manner is to achieve an
elevation of spirit released from the
hold of ego, inspiring growth
through forgetfulness of self.

A spirit is made beautiful by
ever looking to what one can do
to make life more beautiful.

To wake with noble purpose is
the greatest blessing of the day,
and of a life.

Service is the core of higher purpose.
It is what defines it, aiding all needs
within the ambit of spiritual
strength of the devoted servant.

To be born into the world is to be given to the world if realizing the spiritual of human life. Not in an ego sense, but as a vessel of service and love.

When truly committed to making one's life more than just about oneself, what io required is no longer seen as a sacrifice, but a privilege and honor to serve.

The question of the devoted spirit
is not "What is the measure of my
contentment?" but "What is the
measure of my contribution?"

A life of devotion is as expansive
as the distance to where its giving
has reached the lives of others.

The principal insight of a spiritual
awakening is that it is not oneself
that one lives for. (To know this is
to open one's life to the source
of higher wisdom.)

Inner strength becomes tenfold
when turning one's attention away
from oneself and on to a goal that
benefits the needs of the whole.

To be consumed with self is to be
as restricted as the body itself; to
live through selflessness is to have
a spiritual mobility as great as the
universe, free to serve all.

A true expansion of consciousness
is one that realizes that from its
result there is now more to be
given — is always an increase of
generosity, never of greedful
desires to have more.

A spiritual devotion fosters kindness,
compassion, munificence, freedom
from domination of self-preservation
beyond saving oneself for endeavor
that contributes to what the best
of human life is truly about.

Until giving all that one has, a
human being cannot claim to have
done everything that he or she can
do for the world; cannot claim a
devotion rooted in the spiritual.

One is never in the wrong place,
or squandering a moment of time
when doing for the good of others.

A spiritual devotion has nothing
of duplicity behind its offerings.
It is void of furtive schemes and
trickery; it presents no show
to direct attention away from
machinations; it gives selflessly
to the receiver without hidden
fee, asking nothing in return.

To the devoted spirit the gifts one is
given are as spiritual currency to
pay the fare of one's life — not
assumed to be without charge or
obligation, considering it one's
duty to utilize them in ways
that yield purely for the world
what is free of corruption.

It is not only the accepted obligation,
but also the desire of the spiritual
servant to find the way to love
and do the work of love.

The devoted life lives not in a
mindset of day-to-day,
but day for day.

The devoted life opens to the day
and receives its blessings; opens
to the day and gives the fruit
of its blessings.

Where one is doing one's best
in service to the realization
of humankind's best . . . there
is the portrait of spiritual
commitment.

A serious spirituality strives to realize
gifts that realize virtues, uniting in
force to serve the world without
boundaries to the service of giving.

In the enlightened devotion
living and loving are one;
life and purpose
are one.

The noble heart recognizes that it is
a greater honor to serve than to
be served, and that love is only
a word until it is lived.

Devotion does not ask; it does
not wait; devotion Does.

In selfless service is where love can
perform to the fullness of its measure
and extend to its farthest reach.

As the white of a sunray's light
contains all the colors of the
rainbow, so the purity of a
spiritual devotion contains all
qualities of a serviceful love.

When focused on others the
spiritual energy of one's life
increases to the dimension
of the focus.

The best of joy and happiness is
experienced through a devotion
that never moves one to muse
over personal joy and happiness.

Human growth doesn't become substantive until it turns away from the personal and on to the universal, which transpires through a growing concern for the wellness of the whole that is greater than for oneself.

Some say, "It is love I need," and
stop. Others say "It is love that
I need to give," and proceed
to give of love.

The spiritual life is mindful of
what it sends out to life, wanting
only to add to its light.

A spiritual devotion never needs to
reassess its mission or reasons for its
actions, ever operating with a heart
of benevolence toward objectives
that are helpful to the world.

Event or circumstance has no
influence on the dedication of
those guided by the higher nature.
No matter the trends of the day
that are followed, they continue
to address the needs of the world
however they are able.

As the spiritual life works in service
for the good, it gains in its power
to promote goodness.

Never does the sentiment that
one has done enough enter
a spiritual consciousness.

When a task is completed the
devoted spirit moves on to the next,
not waiting for reward.

To be adding more to life than
taking from life is to be on
the noble journey.

A distinction of the devoted life
is that it is ever demanding of
itself without demanding for itself,
and never assumes that it deserves
more than what it is given.

Who live with higher purpose
have a persistent drive to draw
as near to spiritual perfection as
they can; to do and be their best in
mind, heart and spirit.

The devoted life cares not
to feel important, but to
do what is important.

Humble and reserved is the life
of devotion, though as free as a
human life can be in its service.

Humility is not weak, or insecure;
it has faith in its strength; enough
so that it is without care to impose it
on others; content to go unnoticed,
yet always ready to be of service to
someone in need who is open
to what it has to give.

From spiritual love comes the
deepest power, for here there is
freedom from all yearnings
to hold power.

A spiritual life is not imprisoned by
ego, is not engrossed with ambitions
of a worldly character, hence liber-
ated to address the evils of the world
without fear or inhibition.

Devotion is determined, patient,
persevering in goals that advance
the spiritual progression of
humankind.

Devotion is filled with an inspiration
to do what is right, which raises the
insight that wholeness of one cannot
be achieved without concern for
the plight of the whole.

When principles are honored
they cannot fail to manifest
positives in the world.

To love profoundly is to not be
concerned with whether or not
one is being loved, but to do
the work of love.

For the noble of heart
it is always about consideration
for others, always about more
than just oneself.

The rule of love is giving.

The devoted life avails to elevate
all the life it can; gives all
the life that it can.

Those who make the most of their lives
in the deepest sense spend of them
only the portion for themselves
that is necessary, and never place
self-survival before higher principle.

When the spiritual life receives
it passes on whatever of the gift
or offering that it may to help
ease the burden of another.

A spiritual devotion sees to present
needs with a love and compassion
whose source is of the infinite.

There are those who don't believe
in any religious description of the
Divine, yet do a divine work; and
those who profess to believe, yet
fail to commit to such work.

The compassionate word is heard
most clearly when accompanied
by the compassionate deed.

Each selfless act adds something of
beauty to the heart of humanity.

The enlightened devotion is void
of attachment, giving for the
sake of giving; loving for
the sake of loving.

A spiritual presence is sensitive
to not being an obstruction to
others, but rather a font of
spiritual nourishment to help them
in their passage through life.

To give anytime, anywhere,
whenever possible, to anyone in
need of something that one can
provide . . . here, the spirit of light
luminates with love of the divine.

The higher devotion works to bring
one closer to the divine source;
works to bring all of humanity
closer to the divine source.

To keep love flowing one must love
most the source from which it flows.

A life cannot be of love
that is not filled with love.

It is they who are ever filled
who are ever giving.

Devotion is the great joy, the great
freedom, central to the evolution
of human aspiration.

No life can know a greater spiritual
health than the life of selfless service.

Whatever good one can do for others
must come from a purity of heart
free of selfish motive if it is to have a
moral nature, which is the only place
where goodness that is true can be
cultivated and given to another.

The love of devotion is wanting what
is right and good for others, not
wanting from them to further
an agenda at their expense, with
no regard for their loss.

Where selfish interests are absent
from human relations, there
wisdom of a higher order will be.

Love, wisdom, truth are ever
present where the best of
life is present.

Not to hold power over others, but
that they be empowered by union
with the spiritual of their lives is
the hope of the spiritual life.

Without spiritual realization neither
the life nor contribution within one's
power to achieve can be achieved,
nor can any step forward be made
that will not fade or be erased,

Even a small degree of selfishness
can prevent the manifestation of
many good things.

Baseness of all kinds can never be naturally outgrown. They must be overcome through awareness and commitment to defeat them, thus opening the way to transcendence.

With no conscious connection to
the spiritual even the most
adept of minds confined to the
earthly realm of the temporal
can only serve the base.

Everything good and noble in the
human world has come to be or has
been sustained by love and courage
of the spiritual of human-being.

A human life cannot be anything
but lost in all its endeavors until
its focus is on other than itself;
can know purpose that generates
substance and meaning only by
doing for what is more
than itself.

Not always sure of the precise
destination, though certain of
the direction is the life
of higher devotion.

It is humility that births the promise
of true and noble character and
keeps virtue and principle in play.

The light of devotion is its crown,
needing no earthly crown.

In higher devotion there is a major
appreciation for even the minor
blessings of life.

The spiritually devoted could have
nothing of worldly riches and know
that they have enough.

The spiritually devoted do not
concern themselves with how well
life is treating them, only
how well they are treating life.

They ask little to nothing of the
world who are willing to give
most to the world.

Devotion is about *being there*,
fully engaged, tending to the
service at hand with the whole
of one's power to serve.

The noble of spirit are willing to take on whatever will generate more good in the world and make their lives more substantive.

It is noble to live with people, if
one is there to help them. It is noble
to live alone, if the work that is
done in solitude is to benefit others.

One also gives when taking only
what one needs, though able
to take more.

Where humility is absent neither
goodness nor greatness of the
true and profound are present.

The great ascendancy is in the
great opening of surrender
to a higher service.

The devoted of humankind make
of their lives an instrument
to be played in the Divine
Symphony of Life.

A human being cannot be fully
realized without union with what
is greatest of all human life.

Before union with the indestructible
an internal clearing of what bars the
way to its power needs to be made,
the clearing being done by an inner
work, for within is where one must
go to access this deepest and most
reliable source of strength.

In the physical world roads are built
by the labors of some so that many
may then travel upon. In the
spiritual, paths are created as they
are journeyed, all who journey
needing to create their own path
to realize the grace they are
being offered.

For the enlightened spirit it is a
duty to correct in one's life what is
able to be corrected, believing in a
responsibility to not be harmful to
others and live as high a standard
of life as one can live, replacing
whatever selfishness there is
with compassion, whatever
darkness, with light.

The devoted life turns away from
what would hinder or take from the
development of its best, understanding that without discipline and
fortitude there is no chance
for a life transcendent.

There is only so much time to develop the gifts one is given and make them of some benefit to the world . . . (this discernment ever at the forefront of the spiritual mind).

Rewards of the temporal are of no
import to the life of devotion.
(Nor does it anticipate any
heavenly reward.)

A practiced faith is a selfless, active
love — if it is truly of the spiritual.

Of more importance than the
religion that someone lives by
is the measure of spirituality
through which he or she lives.

In something of an inner monastery
do the devoted live, yet a spiritual
work is done by them inside and out
with firm commitment, wanting
to help all.

A spiritual sentience ever prepares
for the reception and creation of
wisdom; for the reception and
creation of beauty and love.

The spiritually devoted are also part
artist, for not only do they know
the purpose of their lives,
but also create it.

Devotion is created within, grows
from within, and gathers the
harvests to be given.

The life of devotion commits itself
daily to its purpose and accepts
what evolves with gratitude,
and gives of it what is useful
to give, with gratitude.

On its feet, serving with reverence,
not on its knees extending praise
is where the devoted life reveals
the sincerity of its love.

Only what holds to nothing
can hold nothing back of all
that could be given — such
is the spiritual devotion.

The devoted life seeks not to be
followed, but to bring what it can
to others that is of the spiritual.

It is by serving the best that is
granted to humankind that one
can be of true service to others.

Without spiritual connection,
human connection is not possible.

A mature compassion requires an understanding of the sorrows of the world, yet this demands a reflection that cannot be acquired simply by engagement and observation of others; it also needs contemplation of a kind that can only be known in solitude.

The temporal eye cannot see, the
temporal ear cannot hear, the finite
heart cannot sense profoundly the
dire needs of the world. It is by
sensitivity of the higher nature
that such can be grasped
and rightly acted upon.

The noble of spirit do not
wait for the calling, knowing
it must be labored for,
moving internally toward the
spiritual of human-being.

The way to enlightenment is
narrow indeed, though ever wide
and open must the heart be
to make the journey.

Enlightenment summons the
embracement of higher duty.

What goes with a growing sense of
individual responsibility honed in the
devoted life is a growing awareness
of species-responsibility, i.e., the
recognition that one has a duty to
do whatever is in one's power
to not just make one's life better,
but also the human world better.

Some often ponder whether they
will be missed when they are gone,
not considering how many
opportunities they have missed
to be of aid to others, or make a
difference in someone's life.

What can never be repaid
is standard in the offerings
of an enlightened generosity.

When of a gathering, the noble
of spirit seek not to show what
they can do, but help others to
discover what they can do, and
what they could contribute.

To help another see with greater
clarity, or to think and feel
more deeply is to do something
whose value for a life
cannot be assessed.

A living spirituality is known
by service that is selfless,
compassionate, patient, caring,
pure and unbiased
in its giving.

In the spiritual of humanity an
empathy for all may be achieved.

In service from the higher nature
there is always more that is being
served than the person or matter
directly addressed, for in such
ministration the world is
being served.

Only the spiritual devotion can
know an earthly bestowal
of eternal treasure.

The true servant of the spiritual is of
a nobility beyond all worldly kings.

A life more blessed cannot be than
that of spiritual devotion, for it uses
the present to serve the eternal
good (and what greater purpose
for human life could there be) . . .

The noble of spirit have much care
for what is present, but greater is
their concern for what is to come
after them, knowing that humankind
cannot move forward nor ultimately
survive without a willingness to
strive for advances from which they
will not benefit, working selflessly
in hope for a better tomorrow
that they will not see.

Does not Nature bring forth its bounties, and the sun give its light without expectations of thankfulness or applause? Should not this example be followed, bringing forth one's spiritual bounty to be given to the world without expecting or vying for thankfulness or applause?

The life of higher devotion works
to project as much spiritual light
as it is able before its time of
corporality is through.

Human life cannot be about living
for eternity, but it can be about
connecting to the power of what
will ever be, thereby releasing
the full strength and beauty
of human, spiritual love.

The heart of the spiritual is a
bottomless ocean, a boundless sky,
rich in beauty and light, knowing
a love beyond pain, beyond joy,
beyond time ... a love beyond
even life.

To depart with nothing, having given everything, is to attain all.

One has always the choice to be
good to others, and to life; to live
with kindness and generosity that
through practice can one day come
as naturally as the drawing of breath;
and perhaps to create some beauty,
and reveal some truth; to open, to
learn, to grow in awareness and
love, knowing that before the grave
and beyond it, it is not about "us"
(never about "self"), choosing to be a
vessel of service, living a devotion
that is centered on doing for the
sake of all; to then end one's time
with the blessing of consolation that
the life one has lived could not have
been given to better purpose, nor
guided by higher grace.

ABOUT THE AUTHOR

Carroll Blair is an author of more than twenty
books and the recipient of numerous awards.
His work has been well endorsed and com-
mendably reviewed. Among his titles cited
for distinction are *Through the Shadows*, winner
of the Pacific Book Awards, and *Quarter Notes*,
winner of the Sharp Writ Book Awards.
He is an alumnus of the Boston Conservatory
and lives in Massachusetts.

www.ingramcontent.com/pod-product-compliance
Lightning Source LLC
Chambersburg PA
CBHW021154020426
42331CB00003B/54